tringa solitaria

Tiana Kirk

Presentation by *BookLeaf Publishing*

Web: www.bookleafpub.com

E-mail: info@bookleafpub.com

ISBN: 9789395756761

First edition 2022

DEDICATION

To the man who has permission to break my
heart at least one more time if he wanted to.

ACKNOWLEDGEMENT

Thank you to the people I love and trust most with my words and thoughts, to those who encourage my creative spirals and read every word I write, to those who listen to every voicemail I leave them and ask for clarification through the blubbering. I love and appreciate you endlessly.

PREFACE

There is something so complexly and paradoxically minuscule and colossal about losing people in your life. It is inevitable and can be celebrated, bittersweet, or mourned deeply for any amount of time - sometimes simultaneously.

I think a lot about my feelings and spend an inordinate amount of time trying not to feel them, believing them to be flawed - believing a solitary existence is flawed. There is room for romanticization in all facets of life, though, and one can truly find good in all evil if the desire and drive exist.

How to begin after an ending?

What are the rules for being left?

When does one need to stop reminiscing fondly
on a time in their life they adored and never
wanted to end?

How does one distinguish between mourning,
pining, existing
- not bothering anybody, remembering because
you don't have room to repress?

Why is it okay for you to adopt my mannerisms
and adapt our language to fit your new life
devoid of my presence,
keep all of the presents and pretend like I don't
play a role
in your emotional state on a day to day basis?

Where do we go from here,
if not on parallel directionless paths
after relinquishing all control to time itself,
dusting our hands of the unnatural disaster we
caused?

Who am I now

with my foundation of the joy, light and love
you brought in excess,
cracking under the weight of knowing
I may never hear the echos of our laughter
in anything but my inevitably faltering memory?

I won't be lonely without you

I have succumbed to Stockholm syndrome
My grief has kept me hostage for years
But I consider her my closest friend
No one gets me like she does
And no one else celebrates me knowing her so
well
I am never judged for being messy or clumsy
Or for my inability to get out of bed for days at a
time

I introduce her to my favourite music, shows,
and people
No one else has fallen under her charms like I
have
So we sit in solitude together
On a couch big enough for twelve

I know the circumstances of our companionship
aren't ideal
Yet I find comfort in her company
And miss her when she is away
And nervously anticipate her arrival
Knowing I am in misery when she is around
But at least knowing that the misery is a constant

in an ever shifting world of possibilities of hurt
and anguish
I am safer with her as my anchor
naively hoping drowning
is our worst fate

Never-ending anniversary reminders

Drank or smoked too much tonight
Can't get to sleep
Each time I close my eyes
I feel full body dizzy like
When you took me on the helicopter ride
When I was scared but laughed instead

You held my hand and I melted
And forgot I was afraid of heights
Probably preferred them at that point
Pausing life and passing smiles
back and forth

I get full days knocked out of me
Like the wind
When your name comes up
In casual conversation with our friends

Conflicting advice that never feels right
When you've gotten on my nerves,
people said "leave" because "people never
change"
But now that you're gone and I cry every day

the same people let me know I have so much to
look forward to
when we meet again, because we won't be the
same

It doesn't feel right to socialize
As if everything is peachy fine
But I've made my world lonely every night
Because your company is all I want
Or think I need to make me feel better
If only temporarily
I leave people on read
If I can be bothered to open the texts
I crave being surrounded by your love
And try desperately to find it
or a suitable replacement
In friends, memories, cool air, the sky

I'm lonely
But I know me
And know there's no one to replace you
So until I stop craving you
Needing you
Thinking of you daily
I'll remain

On the up and up

How fortunate am I
To have so many places touched
firepoker memories
love so hard it hurts
Bear hugs that leave bruises
Walking past a pool we swam in
Well over a decade ago
I never would have thought It'd make me sad

How fortunate am I
To not yet know the full extent
Of all you've touched
I still have so much time
To find
All of the ways I love you

I don't have to say the words to know I feel it
It's in phrases we made up that live on
Smiling at scents and inside jokes
That no one else would think to know
Subconsciously paying more attention
To plants we bought together
Petting the animals for both of us
Just a few little things
In case you never knew

I'll never be able to stop loving you

It's impossible not to think of you
When celebrating other peoples love
I hate myself for my inability
To not love and miss you always
Each second you're away,
I wish you'd wished to stay

I always liked my eyebrows
But you were enamoured and let me know
Compliments like steeping tea
I'll love you long after I'm bitter about it

Overthinking hopeful what ifs

I find it odd and oxymoronic
It refuses to make sense
If you came back I would still be hurt
But wouldn't relate to my thoughts and words
That I haven't been able to stop writing down

I am consumed, all of my time is filled
With my brain, the grief weaver
Spinning poetic purges
Fire with a filter
Burning homes down but it's appealing
To those who don't live there
Keeps others warm
They remove layers of clothing to
Stand even closer

That feels like you've been in the pool
As a kid all day
And you nap in the shade
The heat radiates from inside

Your absence has created life
That works for a living

Will work until it dies
Of old age or suicide
Or a gentle paired walk down
A dusty road to the farm where Ocean drowned

Burn baby burn

I'm so conflicted
I want to be happy
But it's conditional sometimes

August 1st destroyed me
And I knew, going in, that it'd be hard
I'm usually up for a challenge
But I never wanted to partake in this one

How fast has this year sped past me?
I've lost track of my ability to gauge it

I just want to watch the sunrise
- and tell you about it

You keep asking me to close the faucet
As if it's something I control
As if it will stop the love I have for you
From overfilling every oversized mug I own
Alternatively, if it remains open
There must come an end
A drought
No supply, no demand
An unrenewable subscription
Loving you isn't a fad though

Good things still exist
I yearn for autumn
I pine for a crisp bite of apple air
and a chill that a good sweater can fend off
Dressing up, walking to campus
Drinking coffee, feeling like an adult
With her shit together
It's concerning and confusing
and borderline concussive
trying to convince myself that the good still
exists

I know it does, it's just that you made all of
these things better.
Like I was colourblind
going through life enjoying what I had
but you came along, human EnChroma,
and expanded my senses

You left them when you left me and I carry them
around
Laughing at our jokes people say but aren't
making
Watching the ghost racer version of you speed
off on the path I'm stuck on
So I carry them, knowing the power isn't there

But wistfully thinking they might just need a
charge
Maybe they're solar powered
So I spend more time outside than we did
Creating my own little 'stitions

What I think I'm trying to say is that
I want to allow myself to be excited for fall
Without you
The death and decay align with your take on our
tryst –
(pour moi c'est triste)

Maybe if I'd listened to the Stones more when
you put them on I'd know

I want to watch the sunrise before my day begins
- drink coffee on my porch in slippers
I miss romanticizing slow mornings
I heavily anticipate, setting my expectations too
high, knowing I can't win
I want too much but I'd scrap the list and burn it
if you'd join me by the fire

Maybe you shouldn't ask?

Whenever I've had too much to drink and the nauseating feeling washes over me I use all of my remaining energy on not puking and I go to sleep and wake up feeling fine normally.

If I had anything more to drink - water, particularly humid air, one final tequila shot because "you haaaaave to" I would definitely throw up and that would make it worthy of a story and I cannot have any more strikes against my fragile reputation

If I stand still on the fractured ice and distribute my fluctuating weight on it I might just make it as a gradually freezing statue who did not throw up on my friend's floor or yard or toilet

When I have had too much time to myself to think and a nauseating feeling washes over me, I have a glass of wine or smoke half a joint and call someone to force lighthearted conversation or lose myself in a book or tv show while doomscrolling the same four apps on rotation waiting to see something that will hurt my feelings or fulfil my self prescribed need for retail therapy.

In that, I mean I am one "are you okay?" from going to the hospital for 48 hours.

Fantasties

You care that I still love you

You drive past my house or street and feel happy
and sad at the same time - comforted knowing
we are still close in some way, sad that we are
not in most others

You open social media and check in on posts
I've been tagged in or have made and smile with
a twinge of guilt that makes you scroll away for
the same reason

You think I'm beautiful and regret not telling me
more often, remembering the time I tearfully
wished for you to not save the word for our
wedding day.

I am not alone in thinking about or of you every
day

You don't look for excuses to un-memorize me

You are too scared to tell me that you regret the
permanence of your decision

Your parents miss me and talk about me
sometimes, maybe ask if you've seen or spoken
to me recently

You cry on a semi-regular basis because you
miss me and are grieving the loss

You consider losing me to be a painful loss

You are filling your time with as many friends
and faces to distract yourself from being hurt

You have someone in your life that will tell you
their opinion about our relationship, how they
don't think it's a bad idea to try again, and you'll
listen, maybe even consider it

You still love me

Misplacing my lost virginity

Sometimes I wonder if you're kissing other girls
Not even in a real way
I can't exist without dissociating in some form
apparently
Just in a "what does moving on look like to
you?" way
- if you kissed anyone did it make you feel
guilty or nice?
I don't know which I hope for

But I haven't kissed anyone since I kissed you
on April 20th after watching
the last episode of Breaking Bad I probably ever
will
if you don't join me.
And I don't know if it matters to you
I think it'd make you sad
for me

Feels odd to know you so well and not know
what you're up to

I know you so well that thinking about your
normal actions soothes my anxiety still to this

day. Intrusive thoughts of the possibility of you
sending a lengthy cease and desist message are
wiped clean knowing of our mutual loathing of
having serious conversation over text.

I thought about having sex today, as a concept
How fiercely protective I am of my post-you
virginity
How's it's still just a concept
How tangled I get in the endless loops of your
mom's advice for me to allow myself to be "hot
and single" while not believing I am either
I wake up relieved that I haven't kissed anyone
as if it would change who I am as a person and
I'm glad I didn't "sacrifice my integrity" to
"move on" when I clearly don't want to

I will not sacrifice my integrity for your sake

Loose change

People shouldn't be allowed to miss other people
this much
I didn't think to think I might
I don't have many pictures of myself without
you doing my favourite things
torturing myself sorting through the last four
years, scrolling, pretending to be you so it
doesn't hurt as
badly - if at all

Mindlessly select all and delete
unapologetically
only sorry you didn't do it sooner
so the eraser shavings wouldn't fill your desk
and time spent trying to brush them off

I wonder, how close to simultaneous for both of
us, that I went from your forever plus one
- unquestionably
to tedious vacuum fodder
or if you sat on it a while
flipped a coin a few times
before committing to how you'd like to waste
your time from that point forward

respite comes with the pathetic conclusion
that minds are fickle and can change on a dime,
you changed yours once, you could do it twice
right?

What am I supposed to do with that?

We can say hi or even make eye contact
From across the grocery store
And maybe just have a quiet internal sigh
of what ifs and regret
but you came by and assured me
"I don't hate you" as if you knew I wasn't
certain of it
or anything about you anymore

I promised myself the next time
That you offered a hug I'd say no
And mean it
Not able to tell you the withdrawal
Was eviscerating
But I caught myself in a lie
And you caught me in your arms
Unintentionally I leapt into them
Our bodies stuck like magnets
Swaying softly for full minutes

Wasn't until then I knew
Not only could you see a smile
Beneath a mask
But you could feel it
In a trance

Partially abandoned in a fully haunted house

How can I feel you
when looking at photos
Like your ghost comes to life
For a flicker of a moment
Like it wants to stay and is coaxed out of hiding
just to say hi so quietly
If you could hear me I'd plead
Don't be so shy
Stay until just before it hurts
Play chicken with fire
Pull away before it burns
Then go and rest, get well and come back soon
Maybe stay forever, if it hurts more to go
You're always welcome
You could never overstay
But you could stay over
If you ask a little louder
Who am I to say no?

I'm probably allergic to wasps

Sometimes I am stabbed
pain from beautiful memories
stained with your glaring absence
And I wonder if it would hurt you too
if you experienced it

This time I don't even care

I've made soda water hundreds of times
since we moved apart
Made my own ice
in the pink small tray
that you would have loved
- the silicone wouldn't have broken
like our plastic did
I can imagine your joyous childlike movements
Using the tiny pink scoop to chill your beverage
I've even mixed many a cranberry (no sugar
added) soda

But this stings
How I imagine ten vengeful wasps targeting my
heart might feel

I was unpacking recently, finding your things
haphazardly strewn through every box - like you
don't really want to leave
I was resentful at the implication of your
intentions
Accidentally cruel, thinking your presence
provides comfort without the nausea
An arsenic pacifier

I found our glassware
We'd divided the treasure
- the abandoned milk crate of pint glasses

I'm watching the carbon bubbles rise
Mesmerized
Like an old windows screensaver
Can't bring myself to take a sip
Of my favourite drink

I know it will taste like not being loved by you

Bring on the haunt, baby

You're here long after you stopped wanting to be

It should bring comfort but it just makes me sad

Where are you really?

You said you'd love me forever

I promised you'd live in my heart for longer

But you're seeping out into

The new life you want me to build

Without you in it

But I can't manage for a minute

I can throw it all into a bag

Tie it tightly, and with all my strength

Send it soaring into the nearest ocean

But it'd just come back to me

A lazy river boomerang

You come back to me

You're not a lesson I ever wanted to learn

Just a sharp weapon that threatens pain to be
earned

My clumsy hands can't keep hold of it

So it plunges deeper each moment I let it

Why do I let it?

I could just let it go

But I'd still want to know

Where are you really?

Did you imagine you'd be temporary?

Tell me what you think of romance

No wrong answers

Traveling bluer than our suitcase

It's so much more fun to have fun
Travelling together
Two meals

Eating at a restaurant alone is fine
Eating at our restaurant alone is fine
Eating alone at a restaurant on a romantic island
is death
with every silent bite
Every sip of wine
without conversation and laughter
burns going down

It feels irresponsible to be on vacation
with a broken heart
as if there is a bandage big enough
to do the job only a cocoon could

Dr. S said to go out and have fun
Because the sad would be there no matter what
happened or where
She prescribed a dose of "don't be sad"
As I hugged my ex-future mother in law to be
For one of the last times

I wonder what life looks like from the outside in
Without all of the planning
That goes in
To creating what should be fun
But ends up being ticking off the to do list
Created months ago
Anticipation over

But what does it look like to you?

No one knows the reason I booked my trip to
ensure I arrived on the 24th.
I doubt you will even recognize it when it
comes.
Our memories only matter to me

Equally terrifying
What if I'm sad about this forever?
What if I'm not?

house sour house

Newcomers enter what used to be yours
My "home"
I can't bear to call it by its title
It doesn't deserve it yet
I haven't done enough
It's still stained by your name
That once dripped from my mouth
Like honey on an heirloom tufted rug

It's humiliating to have it hanging over my head
A glaring warning to potential lovers, foes or
friends
"Still in love with her ex"

Your name etched in my heart
It's like I'm walking around with a tree trunk of
a splinter in my chest
No one can see it but the pain in my eyes is
evident
On display in not a cute way

the house would be warmed all the same
if we, as a group, had doused it in flames

i'm trying so hard

need ativan to fall asleep
without you in my bed
we couldn't dare to dream
without our feet
resting together
beneath the duvet

so how could you expect me
to be okay?
to function on a day to day?
to not think of you and want to say
come home

you're getting further but I bet I could do it
shout so softly
enticingly
that you might just want to
it's hard to say though
I wish I knew (how)
I could

marathon i couldn't run

we went hiking once or twice
but there is no test for endurance like loving you

still hoping there will be another peak to strive
for
once I've reached the plateau that I never
thought would come
would've walked for the rest of my life up any
hill
no matter how steep
i've always been clumsy
slipping and catching myself comes naturally

now immortalizing my thoughts
even if it's just for me
to read as a future emotional archaeologist
that version of myself is as foreign to my present
self
as so many past selves I can't recall
phases, hair lengths and colours,
fluctuating weights and friends
it's been five months since you said you didn't
think you could be happy anymore
i've held tightly to your words
clenching my fists around them until they bleed

thoughts change all the time
mine do on a second's notice
perhaps the future me who read these entries
will have long since lost the indentations
of my nails in her hands
and gently caresses lotion on the fading scars

always temporarily

not sure if you're aware of or ignoring
the consequences your actions merit

you didn't have to lie
no one forced your lips to part and touch
mine over and over
whispering echoes of always

i find it so odd
your desire to hear about my life now
exclusively second hand
like paraphrasing the great american novel

are you lazy or apathetic to the real thing?
maybe just deliberate illiteracy

how am I to believe happiness or endings exist
when no one wakes me from my post-work-nap
with a kiss?

i always struggled trying to understand
what acts of service meant to you
how they could be translated
to something i could do

it never ended up being enough
but i still think there's something i could've done
or can still do
to make you hear, see, and feel
how much i love you
always

rum and eggnog

I'm not much of a gambler but
I'd bet my life savings
that the sting of missing me
Will be ever so present
Just before christmas n new years

I'd go for broke
Double or nothing
If I could know
What you were thinking

When you collect a single glass
Filled three or four times over again
With what used to be a joyfully
Intoxicating holiday tradition

Maybe I'm projecting
Or just playfully egging you on
To hate our favourite party drink
Of spiced rum and egg nog

it was fun while it lasted

shaking hands and letting go
without really letting go
i've had dreams and nightmares about that
moment
there was nothing to say that could do justice to
the way
we loved each other

i feel as though my brain started
a private competition with itself
and invited me to bear witness
to see how much it can recollect without prompt

intrusively, unconsciously thinking about
our parallel response
to your parents' inquiry
if you were a cat or dog person

verbatim at different times and places
and their approving laughter
we knew each other so well
maybe I just knew you

i can't recall the last time I brought myself a
glass of water before bed

but it used to be our ritual
to hear the ice clinking the glass as we walked
up the stairs
precariously
because we'd filled them too full

is this what moving on feels like?

everyone wants me to be but
i'm not mad I got to experience
the parts of you
that I considered the best
that you felt you needed to grow out of

i had so much fun
i wish it'd lasted longer
embarrassed now to say forever

i hope that no one else ever has to
shake your hand and have you drop theirs
to the tune of
it was fun while it lasted

9 789395 756761